Saffron Chronicles of Uttar Pradesh:

A November Ode

Annapurna Debnath

Ukiyoto Publishing

All global publishing rights are held by

Ukiyoto Publishing

Published in 2024

Content Copyright © Annapurna Debnath

ISBN 9789362694164

All rights reserved.
No part of this publication may be reproduced, transmitted, or stored in a retrieval system, in any form by any means, electronic, mechanical, photocopying, recording or otherwise, without the prior permission of the publisher.

The moral rights of the author have been asserted.

This is a work of fiction. Names, characters, businesses, places, events, locales, and incidents are either the products of the author's imagination or used in a fictitious manner. Any resemblance to actual persons, living or dead, or actual events is purely coincidental.

This book is sold subject to the condition that it shall not by way of trade or otherwise, be lent, resold, hired out or otherwise circulated, without the publisher's prior consent, in any form of binding or cover other than that in which it is published.

www.ukiyoto.com

Firstly, I am grateful to my parents for the precious gift of being raised on the sacred soil of India. Their gift of nurturing me in the culturally rich and historically profound landscape of this nation is a blessing beyond measure. A special thanks goes to my talented cover designer who lent his artistic vision to the creation of my book cover. Your creativity has beautifully encapsulated the essence of my writing, adding depth and allure to its presentation. I extend my sincere appreciation to Ukiyoto Publishing House for their belief in my work and for providing me with the opportunity to share my literary voice with the world. Their dedication to nurturing emerging authors is truly commendable. Lastly, to all the readers who have supported my journey by reading my book, I extend my heartfelt appreciation. Your interest and encouragement have meant the world to me.

When I wanted to understand what is happening today, I try to decide what will happen tomorrow; I look back, a page of history is worth a volume of logic.

~ *Oliver Wendell Holmes*

Contents

Serendipity 1
The Journey 19
Triveni Sangam 35
Train To Mathura 49
Mathura 73

About the Author 81

Serendipity

The sky seemed to hold the promise of rain that day. Mrunal, seated on her wooden wing chair, engaged in a therapy session over a Skype call with her old client, who was diagnosed with bipolar II disorder about a year ago. According to ICD-11, this condition involves intermittent mood swings, including hypomanic and depressive episodes lasting over two weeks.

"Are you following Dr. Jha's prescribed medication?" she inquired.

"Yes. Can I share some updates?" Ms. Mukherjee responded.

"Certainly."

"Ma'am, my sleep cycle has normalized, and the intensity of mood shifts has reduced. Following your suggestion, I've recently joined a music class and slowly shaping the life I envisioned. Your guidance has been instrumental in this transformation."

"I've merely guided you…you've achieved this for yourself. Clap for your progress." Mrunal affirmed.

"Thank you, ma'am."

"By the way, I'll be out of station for my academic duties this Friday. If you need me, text on WhatsApp."

"Sure. Is it for research?"

"No, I've been invited as a guest lecturer."

"Good luck."

"Thank you. Take care."

Mrunal's clinical journey began under Dr. Tarun Kumar Jha's influence after completing her MPhil degree at NIMHANS Hospital, Bangalore. Uncoached, she cracked the UGC Net exam, pursued a Master's at IIT BHU -- a dream portfolio every budding psychologist aims to wrap in their resume. But Mrunal's adolescent dreams sought a different tableau, infused with the nuances of Gothic literature and Indian history. A few lines from Tagore's poem, titled "Shadharon Meye" says,

"I am a girl from the inner court,

You don't know me.

Read your novel, the one unfurled recently –

'The Garland of Withered Flowers'"

This was the essence of young Mrunal at 13, a delicate spirit crafting her haven amid the pages of books, where tales of monumental history whispered from the corners of her school library.

During one of her family trips to Pune when she was in 8th grade, she had eloquently recounted the history of the Shaniwar Wada fort to her parents, skillfully serving as their tour guide. "Teak was sourced from the jungles of Junnar, stone from the nearby quarries of Chinchwad, and lime from the lime-belts of Jejuri. Originally a 7-story structure, it has now been reduced to a skeletal reminiscence of its former grandeur, a consequence of British artillery in 1818. In the 18th century, Shaniwar Wada stood as an epicenter of Indian politics. The enduring stone base of this palace resonates in homage to the Marathas, the warriorhood of the Peshwas, still adorned by the patronage of Chatrapati Sahu Maharaj."

This scenario had left her parents awestruck. Dusk, like a whispered secret, delicately tiptoed along the rays of evening twilight, casting a tender glow over the Bronze Statue of Peshwa Bajirao I, positioned to the north of Dilli-darwaza on the Kashba Peth Road - this ambiance mirrored a reflection of autumn. But her fervor for history gradually faded into the recesses of oblivion as she found a new passion in the realm of behavioral science. Thereby, in the orchestration of life, the only certainty is, indeed, its inherent uncertainty.

Mrunal closed her laptop and kept it beside her wooden pen stand at the edge of her Mahogany desk. After taking a sip of her Darjeeling tea, she pulled the white block-printed chiffon curtains and locked her gaze at the drizzly boulevards of Lake Avenue, dipped in hues of the sombre evening sky of Kolkata. She plugged in her earphones and played "Dhara Hogi" from her playlist, "Threads of classical music." A fusion of rag Brindabani Sarang and Megh Malhar blended with folk music of Rajasthan is enough to stitch the kohl borders of thunder to enjoy a rainy day in India.

"Baaje thare aangan maa
Bundon ka jhankara

Ni aaj thaari nagari maa
Ghir ghir aayo re badal kaala"

Mrunal chose to undertake a shopping expedition to Esplanade, the commercial hub of the city. Its roads exude a pure essence of *"angrezon ka zamana,"* ornamented with buildings that stand as architectural masterpieces from the Colonial era in *Kalikata*. Additionally known as Dharmatala, this locale derived its name from the Dharmaraj temple which has been a revered site of worship for the Dom community for many years, as documented by the journalist and researcher Binoy Ghosh. Taking the blue line metro, Mrunal meandered through the Esplanade Row. She walked through the streets, passing by the Victoria House which is now housing CESC offices and Statesman House- the enduring home of "The Statesman", one of the country's oldest newspapers. She continued past the Metropolitan building, once a British-era department store which still has its original neo-Baroque architecture featuring domes, a clock tower, Corinthian columns, and recessed arched windows, before entering the New Market Area. This

Victorian-style gothic market complex was unveiled to the English populace in 1874 and named after Sir Stuart Hogg. It held a special place in the hearts of the Bengali society of the British era, who affectionately called it "Hogg Shaheb er bajar"—a name still embraced by the locals.

Dharmatala area in British -era, Kolkata.

Mrunal got indulged in a shopping spree. She added a Shantiniketani purse, a Kashmiri shawl, and two sets of Chikan kurta to her curated collection. She then entered Nahoums bakery and selected two minced pie tarts, a brownie cake, and a cheese puff—an enticing combination of Jewish cuisine for her train journey to Allahabad.

After picking up a few more items for her journey, Mrunal wandered down East Esplanade toward Dacres Lane, a well-known food street in central Kolkata, famous for Chitto Babu's chicken stew and dry chilli chicken. This culinary hotspot offers a variety of Indo-Chinese combos like fried rice with chilli chicken, chowmein, and Manchurian, along with Bengali delights such as Bashonti Polau and kosha mangsho (gravy chicken). Mrunal grabbed a plate of rice and paneer from Arun Kaku's "Maa Tara Hotel," renowned for its vegetarian cuisine across the city. The drizzle resumed as she walked towards the Metro Station, catching a sight of the elegant white arched gate of Raj Bhawan on her left —an architectural gem that Lord Curzon once praised as unmatched among Government Houses worldwide. In the untimely November rain, this neoclassical structure carried the fragrant whispers of Central Calcutta's rich colonial history.

Mrunal checked her phone upon entering the metro. It had been untouched for the past 3 hours, and as expected, numerous messages awaited her on WhatsApp, a common occurrence for a psychotherapist. A notification in the panel caught her attention, displaying, "Mail from University Of Allahabad." With a smile, she opened it to review the details of the seminar she was invited to as a guest lecturer by the psychology department of Allahabad University for addressing the topic, "Neurological Basis of Human Memory." While she checked the attachments of the mail and messages from her clients, an announcement called out,

"Agla Station Rabindra Sarobar, Platform Dayein Taraf."

While juggling with the house keys and shopping bags, Mrunal's phone buzzed in her denim jeans – it was her mom's call.

'How's it going, Shona? Ate dinner?'

'Just returned home Maa. Got some stuff for the trip.'

'You don't seem to care of yourself. Look at your face in the recent snaps… you appear to have shed some weight. This is why you need someone to watch over you. Is there someone on your mind, or…'

'Maa, marriage isn't in the cards right now. I'm at the pinnacle of my career, aspiring for greater financial independence. Perhaps, I'll consider it after a year.'

'You're 30 already. When's this 'year' ending?'

'Celebrities get married even at 40!'

'Do you even resemble one?'

Both chuckled.

'I miss you, Maa. How's Binoy Mama? I'll soon make my way to Mumbai to be with you. The plan to shift is in motion. Actually, joining a government college as an assistant professor in another state is challenging, but clinical practice poses no difficulty…'

"You're diligent, my Shona. You'll overcome this. We miss you too. Also, pay a visit to Kalighat temple and offer a puja for all of us. Tomorrow is Amavasya, a propitious day, I believe. Show your gratitude to Maa Kali for your first offer as a guest lecturer.'

'I'll go in the morning. I promise.'

'Send me snaps.'

'Sure. I need to freshen up now, Maa. Feeling quite tired.'

'Rest well. I love you.'

'Love you too, Maa. Bye.'

Mrunal placed her wet umbrella next to the ebony shelf in her drawing room. Her eyes landed on the Kalighat Patachitra above it—a cat with a Vaishnavite mark stealing a crayfish, a Bengali satire from around 1940, passed down from her great grandfather. Within the walls of her home, this painting stands as a venerable antique, echoing an era when this craft was pioneered by a group of skilled "patuas" near the Kalighat Kali Temple. Beyond its mythological narratives and depictions of Hindu deities, these artworks also serve as historical snapshots, chronicling the societal shifts during the 19th and early 20th centuries. Victoria and

Albert Museum website mentions that the artworks in the museum have been "created and collected over a period of 100 years from 1830s to the 1930s"

In the early 19th century, Calcutta had blossomed into a vibrant economic hub through the commercial endeavors of British and European settlers, attracting hopeful immigrants. The southern enclave of the city, graced by the Kalighat Temple, emerged as a magnetic destination for pilgrims, curious visitors, and locals. Within this dynamic landscape, artisans and craftsmen, notably the skilled patuas from rural Bengal, including regions like Midnapore and the 24 Parganas, seized the opportunity to showcase their talents. These patuas, rooted in the ancient tradition of patachitra, painted intricate narratives on expansive scrolls of cloth or handmade paper, sometimes exceeding lengths of 20 meters. The term "patuas" stems from the sections called "pats" in these artworks. Interestingly, the roots of this group of traveling folk painters can be traced back to the thirteenth-century text, the Brahma Vaivarta Purana, adding a historical depth to their artistic journey. But the fame and popularity of Kalighat paintings gradually faded in the early 20th century. The proliferation of affordable printed reproductions inundated the markets, marking a steady decline in the original art form. It is this very aspect that elevates this painting in Mrunal's home to the status of an antique. It encapsulates an era when these artworks radiated authenticity, prompting her to safeguard it with utmost care.

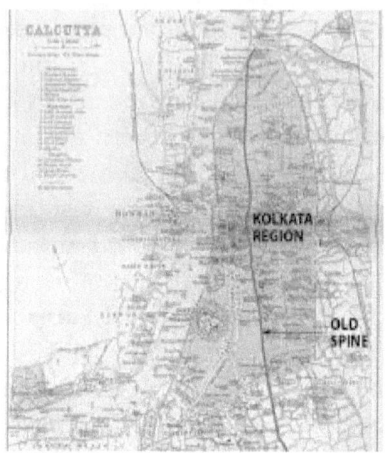

1st map of the entrance of Patuapara.

Traditional houses of patuas

The following morning, around 8:30, Mrunal set out in an Uber towards Kalighat. This sacred site, a shaktipeeth, holds historical significance as the namesake of the city. Acquired by the colonial government in 1758 after the fall of Siraj-ud-daulah, the last independent Nawab of Bengal, from Mir Jafar, this area comprised of several villages, collectively known as Dihi Panchannagram. Kalighat, initially a part of this ensemble, was considered a suburb beyond the Maratha Ditch. Originally named Kali-Kshetra, it is widely believed to be the origin of Kalikata, eventually evolving into Calcutta and then Kolkata. The cab paused at a signal near Rashbihari Avenue, alongside a vintage yellow tram heading towards Tollygunge. Mrunal recalled her school days, commuting in these trams and wished for the restoration of their past glory, especially after reading about the Calcutta High Court's efforts to revive them.

The first horse-drawn trams in India operated a 2.4-mile route between Sealdah and Armenian Ghat Street in the 1870s. The Calcutta Tramway Company, established in London marked a significant milestone by laying meter-gauge horse-drawn tram tracks from Sealdah to Armenian Ghat via Bowbazar Street, Dalhousie Square, and Strand Road. Inaugurated by Vice Roy Lord Ripon around 1880, this route played a pivotal role in the city's transportation history.

A 19th century horse-driven tram in Calcutta.
Wooden Tram Of Kolkata

The car came to a halt along the main road, just a 5-minutes' walk from the temple complex. Mrunal purchased a traditional "dala," crafted with twigs and shal pata, containing sindur, alta, hibiscus flowers, pera, and bangles for the deity. Above the temple's atchala roof, the sun gleamed brightly, illuminating its metallic silver surface painted with vibrant bands of red, yellow, green, and blue colors. After waiting in a line for 30 minutes, the long-awaited Darshan of Dakshina Kali finally happened. Dakshina Kali's name is believed to be derived from the Sanskrit verses of Adya Stotra, specifically...

"Kaalikaa Vangadeshe Cha Ayodhyaayam Maheshvari."

The striking black stone idol has fiery eyes, a long golden tongue, and four hands – two holding a scimitar and the severed head of the asur king 'Shumbha'. The scimitar symbolizes divine knowledge, while the asura head represents human ego. Human ego, as defined by Sigmund Freud, works upon the reality principle for satisfaction of Id impulses by either delaying or postponing them in accordance with reality without checking whether the impulses are morally right or wrong. Hindu chronicles depicting clashes between positive and negative forces subtly convey the conflict between conscience and wrongful motives. The idol's remaining two hands form the abhaya and varada mudras, representing blessings.

After a meditative pause in the Nat Mandir complex adjacent to the Kali Temple, Mrunal departed for Gokhale College, to deliver her afternoon lecture.

"Alfred Adler's life mirrored his psychological theories, with early health challenges such as rickets, which shaped his perspective. Stricken by this condition until age four, he emerged physically weakened, instilling resilience that fueled his determination to prove himself. This theme persisted in his later work, influencing theories on compensation and the pursuit of superiority in individual psychology. Despite health struggles, Adler rose to prominence, co-founding the Vienna Psychoanalytic Society and laying the groundwork for his distinctive psychological theories. In the upcoming lecture, I'll explain the concepts of superiority and inferiority complexes."

Concluding her lecture, Mrunal walked to the departmental staffroom adjacent to the laboratory or lecture hall. A heartfelt conversation unfolded with Dr. Mitra.

"Best of luck, Mrunal, for your upcoming seminar in Allahabad. When is your train?"

"Tonight, ma'am. I have to head home early."

"Absolutely. Have a safe journey… But may I share something with you?"

"Of course. Please do."

"I see a peculiar reflection of Professor Adler's life in yours. I clearly remember your battles with asthma during your college days, managing inhalers and medications. Despite health hurdles, you persevered, submitting medical reports for your absences, and dedicatedly studying in the library on days when you were able to attend the classes Your mother once told me about your persistent health struggles since your childhood, like. Enduring weekly painful injections for dust allergy…. Yet, you managed everything…your life your career. Literally everything with such brilliance!!!I extend my heartfelt blessings for your upcoming lecture at AU. Best of luck."

Mrunal touched Dr. Mitra's feet and departed for her home.

Turning right from Harish Mukherjee Street, she made her way towards Rabindra Sadan Metro Station. She passed by Nandan cinema, the cultural centre of Kolkata founded by Jyoti Basu, the former Chief Minister of Bengal and inaugurated by the Oscar-winning film director, Satyajit Ray. It had remained a significant venue for the Kolkata International Film Festival until 2010. Today, Nandan stands as the guardian of "bangaliyana," hosting vibrant art and music festivals, the soulful cadence of Sufi and Baul performances, captivating exhibitions, and the entrancing allure of various dance and drama spectacles. With every delicate sip of "bhar er cha", bite of fish fry and moghlai Paratha, Nandan is still a testament to the enduring beauty of the city's cultural legacy.

Mrunal completed packing her last suitcase and left for Howrah Station in a yellow Ambassador taxi. The Ganges reflected the golden glow of Howrah Bridge, weaving a poetic charm over the City of Joy. The distant chimes of Dakshineshwar's Sandhya arati echoed as she stepped into the station. She scanned the platform display board to check the platform number of the train and if it was on right time. As she waited for the train, she flipped through Shri Aurobindo's

"Karakahini" when suddenly an announcement was made for her train which said,

" Yatri Gan Kripaya Dhyan De.

Gari sankhya ek, do, tin, ek, ek, Netaji Express, platform number 9 se 21:55 par rawana hogi. Dhanywaad."

The Journey

Mrunal has always cherished the simplicity of train travels over flights and AC compartments. Since childhood, she has always found some bizarre peace in the blue middle bunk of general bogies and falling asleep to the gentle hum of the train. Waking up to hawkers' calls at 7:00 am in the morning. she would discover a world cloaked in fog, draping silver over lush green paddy fields outside. Whenever the train made a halt, small Mrunal, holding her father's hands, would step onto stations for buying fruits, a Ludo board, magazines, newspapers, chiklees, cookies and biscuits. Her anticipation to board the train early was fueled by a fear of delays and the possibility of missing it's departure.

"Baba, please hurry up... Else the train will leave."

"No maa, it won't. Let me buy lays for you and your mother. You love the green ones na?"

"Yes baba."

Only Bengali daughters can savor the unique warmth of being called "Maa" by their fathers.

As the train left Howrah, a sequence of these events flickered in Mrunal's mind. The train began to gather hawkers from the next station, making their way through the confined pathways of the general coaches. To Mrunal, the coolies and hawkers of Indian Railways carry responsibilities more than goods within their luggages and baskets, which are often discarded by the privileged along their journey. They are up to serve people even when the clock falls asleep. The earthen vessels at railway tea stalls seem to hold stories of their worries and hopes. Their skin is indeed a mirror, which never denies to show the actual weight of life.

Mrunal enjoyed a cup of coffee and the minced pie tart she had packed from Nahoums last day. She shared the extra tart with a girl sitting next to her, busy playing Candy Crush on her mother's phone. The exchange continued as Mrunal offered pastries, cakes, and kalighat's peda prashad from her tiffin box to the Marwari family, fostering a lively conversation in the fleeting air.

"Are you traveling alone?" inquired the girl's mother.

"Yes, I've been solo traveling since my university days,"

"Where are you travelling to?"

"Allahabad"

"Oh, for a family function or something?"

"No, I'm a professor. I have a lecture at Allahabad University on Monday."

"A professor at such a young age, commendable!"

"I'm also a clinical psychologist. Here's my card."

"Psychiatrists are the one who treat abnormal people na?"

"Haha, no. Psychiatrists have an MBBS degree and can prescribe medicines. Psychologists work alongside them, offering counseling and therapy. All three are crucial for treating mental health issues."

"I graduated from Jogomaya Devi College with an Honors degree in history. I don't have a hifi wala profession like yours. I'm a housewife, happily raising my daughter. But I do Phad paintings in my free time."

"Being a housewife, especially a mother, is the most priceless profession on Earth."

"You sound like those highly intellectual Bengali girls"

Mrunal smiled at her,

"Haha, thank you. But what are Phad paintings? I've never heard of them before."

"Phad paintings are basically scroll paintings created on cloth, representing a unique art form which originated in Rajasthan. Initially, they illustrated the performances of Bhopa singers, who were priest-singers in Rajasthan. These paintings have got distinctive styles and patterns, and gain immense popularity for their vibrant colors and historical themes. The Phad of Bhagwan Devnarayan holds the title of being the largest among the popular Pars of Rajasthan. Devnarayan ji is revered as an incarnation of Lord Vishnu by the locals Rajputs. Another notable Par painting is Pabuji Ki Phad. Pabuji is worshipped across Rajasthan and Gujarat. The base for these paintings is crafted from Khadi, soaked overnight, dried, and treated with primer. Male artisans then use a stone device called "Mohra" for burnishing. They employ a flat perspective and bright colors. "

"Do you have any picture of your paintings?"

"Yes, wait."

She scrolled through her gallery and unearthed 2 pictures.

"I made this one on canvas. It depicts Rasleela. These figures are Shyam ji and Radharani, and the remaining ones are the Gopis."

Before Mrunal's eyes, a stunning painting on a red canvas unfurled, adorned with six vibrant colors – red, peach, blue, yellow, green, and pink. The traditional ghunghat and ghagras of Radharani and the Gopis were meticulously layered with red and yellow hues, complemented by blue lace and golden embroidery of circles along their length. The depiction showcased two of them fanning the deities seated on a golden jhula, accompanied by a traditional Rajputi Pankha adorned with red and yellow borders, set against a floral pattern of the cloth. This scenery unfurled beside the blue waters of the Yamuna, where pink lotuses floated. Two other figures in the painting played the Mridangam and Sitar.

The lady swiped to the next painting, which portrayed a scene from the Ramayana. Here, Shri Ram and Mata Sita were seated on their royal throne beneath a majestic chhatri, while Hanumanji humbly sought their divine blessings.

"I wish I could hold these paintings. They're truly priceless. Keep creating such wonders."

"Thank you. Do you paint too?"

"No, but I derive immense joy from witnessing such beauty. My frequent visits to art exhibitions at Birla Sabhagar, Nandan, and ICCR add on to it. By the way, where are you travelling to?"

"Vindhyachal, to the temple of Ma Vindhyavasini. Its a shaktipeeth."

"I've heard tales of that temple. On every Saturday my grandmother would recite the verses of Durga Saptashati, wherein the temple found mention."

"Indeed. I need to wake up before the train enters Mirzapur.. Have to sleep now."

"It was lovely talking to you. I learnt a lot of new things."

Both of them shared warm smiles and ascended to their bunks.

A Few Phad Paintings depicting: Devnarayan ki phad, Maharas and a scene from the Ramayana

Mrunal called her mother before going to bed or 'bunk', after the tiring day.

"I fail to understand why you still opt for general bogies. You certainly earn enough for a more comfortable journey, don't you?"

"Maa... I simply don't enjoy AC coaches. They're rather dull."

"And what if you catch cold? I'm quite sure..You haven't packed a monkey cap. Atleast drape something around your neck and head before going to sleep.."

"I've a thin katha. Don't worry. By the way, I met an extraordinary lady today..my co-passenger... She's a painter specializing in creating Rajasthani Phad paintings during her free time.. However, much like you, she prioritizes nurturing her child over it.. She's going for a pilgrimage to Vindhyachal with her husband and daughter."

"Why doesn't she pursue this professionally?"

"Life and it's circumstances maybe... You know ma, she reminded me of that lady of Aunt Jennifer's Tigers…"

"Tigers? Oh the one written by Adrienne Rich?"

"I feel her life shares a striking resemblance with the second stanza of that poem…..

'Aunt Jennifer's finger fluttering through her wool

Find even the ivory needle hard to pull.

The massive weight of Uncle's wedding band

Sits heavily upon Aunt Jennifer's hand.' "

"Hmm. I get you. Anyway, go to sleep now…"

"The network is poor too… good night maa. I'll call you after I reach Allahabad"

As she adjusted her backpack and air pillow, a few lines from Ajitesh Bandopadhyay's Bengali play 'Nana Ronger Din' echoed in her mind:

"The one who has embraced art, Kalinath, transcends the confines of aging, solitude, and illness. With laughter that echoes

in defiance of mortality, the artist elegantly persists in their creative odyssey."

At 3:30 in the silent midnight, Mrunal woke up to a hushed conversation of the TT with someone likely to be dozing off in his bunk by mistake. She looked at her phone to check the time, and then drew open the window beside her bunk, the train was at Hazaribagh station. Mrunal had once read an amazing award-winning travel memoir titled "Tales of Hazaribagh" authored by poet Mihir Vatsa. In the canvas of her mind, the hills whispered, forests murmured, and lakes shimmered, conjuring a spell of nature's beauty over the Chhotanagpur plateau.

Mrunal again woke up to her 6 a.m. alarm. While brushing her teeth, she stood by the gate for some fresh air. The train arrived at Gaya Junction, bringing back memories of her sixth-grade trip to the place with her mom and grandma. Back then, her mom used to work as a freelance writer from home and saved money for their yearly pilgrimages.

Gaya is about an 8-hour bus ride from Kolkata. Because Mrunal's grandma couldn't handle railway overbridges, they decided on an overnight bus journey to the city. As the hands of the clock approached 6 am, the bus entered the Gaya district, winding through the bylanes of Magadh. Nature painted its masterpiece through them— lush fields engaging in a gentle ballet, trees narrating ageless tales, and mud houses embellished with beautiful wall murals, most of them depicting hooded cobras, the sun and figures of women offering water to tulsi. Each mud-bricked canvas whispered stories of a timeless connection between earth and art.

"Take a look outside, Mrunal." Her mother said. "Perhaps this was the very road through which Samrat Ashoka and Bindusara traveled, maybe this area was once shrouded in dense forests and frequented by the rajvanshis for their hunts."

The bus finally arrived in Gaya city at 7 in the morning. The family opted for an auto to reach Bharat Shevasram Sangh, an organization founded by the patriot saint Acharya Swami Pranavanandaji Maharaj. This place still provides affordable accommodation and Satvik meals for pilgrims, tourists, and monks.

"Bhaiyaji, can you take us on a tour around Gaya? What would be the charge?" Mrunal's mom asked the auto driver.

"It depends on either the kilometers or hours of your travel,"

Her mother assured him saying, "I'll pay you 100 rupees per hour, and I'll set a timer on my mobile for accuracy,"

"Sure. When would you like to start?" asked the auto driver.

"Maybe around 9. Do you know any good place for having breakfast?"

"There's a good hotel right beside the Bharat Shevasram Sangh and a tea stall attached to it, selling really zayekedar kulhad chae,"

Mrunal found solace beyond their chatter; her eyeballs danced in excitement as a herd of goats crossed the road. In the rustic scenery of Bihar, cows grazed on verdant fields with their calves by their side.. Meanwhile, the sun rose majestically above the buildings, casting a spell of harvest seasons over the fields of Gaya.

After drinking a glass of sattu ka sharbat and Gaya's famous muli ka Paratha, the family set out for the tour.

"Bhaiyaji, where are you taking us first?", Mrunal's mom asked the driver.

" Vishnupada mandir", the driver answered.

"Do you know its history? Like who built it, and what is its significance?"

"Actually, this mandir holds the origin of Gaya's name. It is constructed on the site where Bhagwan Vishnu is said to have vanquished the demon Gayasura. Hence, Gaya is derived from Gayasura. The temple features a 40-cm footprint of Lord Vishnu carved into a block of basalt known as Dharmasila, preserved from the moment when the deity stepped on Gayasura's chest before subduing him. Legend has it that Shri Ram and Sita Maiya visited this temple. It was later rebuilt by Ahilyabai Holkar, the queen of Indore, who brought skilled craftsmen from Rajasthan. Crowned by a 50-kilo gold flag, generously donated by a devotee named

Govind Sen, the temple also holds the visitation legacy of Chaitanya Mahaprabhu."

"You're such a history buff!"

"No, no, madamji. I've grown up hearing these stories from my dadiji,"

As the auto stopped outside the temple complex, Mrunal"s grandma opted to remain inside with the driver due to her difficulty in climbing the steep staircase.

Mrunal and her mom placed rose petals and white lotuses encircling Lord Vishnu's footprint, decorated with nine sacred symbols like the shankha, chakra, and gada, within a radiant silver basin. Transitioning from this moment, they continued with their journey towards the Mangala Gauri temple—the shaktipeeth where, according to the Devi Bhagwat Purana, Mata Sati's breasts fell on Earth. The next destination was Sita Kund, a placid spot nested along the banks of the Falgu River, where Mata Sita bestowed pinda to her father-in-law, Raja Dasharath, harmonized with the timeless flow of the river. Over there, Mrunal witnessed the solemn flames of chitas burning on the riverbank, their ethereal dance transforming into wisps of smoke, flawlessly merging with the evening air.

The Vishnupada Mandir, falgu river and few pictures of Gaya from the top of Bramhayoni Hills.

As the train departed from Gaya station, a cascade of these childhood memories flashed in front of Mrunal's eyes, intertwining with the lines of Tin Paharer Koley, penned down by Shakti Chattopadhyay. Mrunal's senior secondary Bengali teacher, Ronjaboti ma'am had posted it on her WhatsApp status... the lines said....

"Lost in whichever direction the path may roam,

A path awaits, leading towards water's mournful foam.

Beyond the woodland's grasp, in realms of the mind's decree,

Echoes of dreams flutter amid the whispering tree.

Slowly, the eastern sky unveils its tender glow,

Cloaking three hills in verdant robes they bestow.
Can life persist with such ease in a fragile frame?"

Mrunal exchanged goodbyes with the family as they got down at Mirzapur. The train hustled through dark tunnels and steel bridges. Meanwhile, she got immersed in an open-eyed meditation, feeling deeply connected to the beauty of rural Uttar Pradesh, enjoying the refreshing November breeze caressing her hair.

"Dyed in the hues of bashfulness and the deep saffron vermilion,
In attire of the cowherd, painted against the canvas of the sky, is, a celestial secret."

She enjoyed Hemanta Mukherjee's timeless tunes from Sa Re Ga Ma Karvan on YouTube while reading Karakahini. As the train slowed down after an hour, a distant announcement filled the air.

"Yatri gan, kripaya dhyan de, gari sankhya ek do tin ek ek Howrah se Kalka jane wali, Netaji Express, platform number 3 pe padhar rahi hai, dhanywaad."

A yellow board at a distance read,

"Welcome to Allahabad."

Triveni Sangam

Mrunal being an adventurous traveler with a fearless spirit, has always got drawn to the tantalizing offerings of street-side cuisine, over Swiggy or Zomato. Her lodging choices reflect a penchant for simplicity and authenticity, favoring the ambiance of Ashrams and Dharmashalas over the opulence of luxury hotels. With an insatiable curiosity for new experiences, she gets absorbed with the pulse of unfamiliar locales while walking through the lively streets and chowks, to interact with the locals and foster a sense of belongingness. This is what influenced her decision to stay at the Bharat Shevasram Sangh in Allahabad instead of any guest house.

Here, amidst the chants of Vedic hymns and beauty of sunflower-bedecked surroundings, she discovers a unique sanctuary- a perfect respite resonating with the rich spiritual roots of Prayag. This historical embroidery intricately weaves together the spiritual legacies of Vedic traditions, the grandeur of Mughal influences, and the echoes of colonial heritage.

"....multitudes upon multitudes of the old and weak and the young and frail enter without hesitation or complaint upon such incredible journeys and endure the resultant miseries without repining." This line was mentioned by Mark Twain after visiting the Kumbh Mela of Triveni Sangham in 1895. The city finds its earliest reference as one of the world's oldest known cities in Hindu texts and has been venerated as the holy city of Prayāga in the ancient Vedas. Prayagraj was also known as Kosambi in the late Vedic period, named by the Kuru rulers of Hastinapur, who developed it as their capital. Kosambi was one of the greatest cities in India from the late Vedic period until the end of the Maurya Empire, with its occupation continuing until the Gupta Empire. Since then, the city has been a political, cultural and administrative centre of the Doab region. The history of the name of this region also stretches far and wide. The location at the confluence of Ganges and Yamuna rivers has been known in ancient times as Prayāga, which means "place of a sacrifice" in Sanskrit (pra-, "fore-"+ yāj-, "to sacrifice"). The Mughal emperor Akbar visited the region in 1575 and was so impressed by the strategic location of the site that he ordered a fort be constructed. The fort was constructed by 1584 and called Ilahabas or "Abode of Allah", later changed to Allahabad under Shah Jahan during the golden age of India. Shaligram Shrivastav claimed in Prayag Pradip that the name was deliberately given by Akbar to be construed as both Hindu ("ilaha") and Muslim ("Allah").

Mrunal hired a horse-drawn Tonga stationed just beyond the Ashram gates, ready to explore the route to the Sangam and wind through the charm of the city. Cloaked in sophistication, she wore a light purple muslin kurti, a canvas alive within chikan kari's floral embroidery and delicate lace. Her attire was a subtle ode to Begum Nur Jahan, the lady who had introduced chikanri to Indian bazaars during the reign of Jahangir.

As she looked into the mirror for completing her final look with a stone bindi, a few lines from Amir Khusro's poetry, "Sakal Ban" played in the backdrop of her mind,

"Phool rahi sarson,

Sakal ban, tesu phoole ambuwa baure

Gori karat shingar"

Two beautiful brown horses pulled the Tonga through the narrow lanes of Prayag, while sunlight filtered through the leafy canopy of trees. The carriage paused near the Triveni Sangham, amidst the tents of boatmen and jatadhari sadhus. Mrunal purchased a silver foiled container with a diya nested among rose petals and a packet of puffed rice while walking towards the boat stand. As the boat gently moved along the fast-flowing waters of the Ganga, the sun's rays bathed everything in its warmth. It was November, and a gentle breeze carried the chill of the river as it mingled with the air. A group of beautiful white birds flew around the boat and some of them gracefully swimmed through the water. Though the Saraswati River might have vanished, it seemed as if its spirit lived on through these birds, acting as guardians of the Earth. Mrunal fed them the packet of puffed rice, like pilgrims on other boats.

"These birds come from Siberia every year around this time and stay till February.", the naowala initiated a conversation with Mrunal.

"I see, Migratory birds!", she added.

"Ji madamji. Would you take a dip into the water? Its Purna kumbha tirtha afterall you know."

"Let's see. But I'll surely do Surya pranam since I've heard that Prayagraj is also called Argha Kshetra. But why is it called Purna Kumbha? I thought that it was Banaras?"

" Bramhadev had himself chosen this land to perform the Prakrista Yagya at the beginning of creation and he considered this place to be the king of all Tirthas. This is the reason why you'll hear pilgrims calling it 'Tirtha raj.'

"Hmm. That is interesting."

"In the puranas, it is also mentioned that once Indradev was carrying the Amrit Kalash when a scuffle broke out and four drops were spilled which fell over four different places, Prayagraj, Haridwar, Nasik and Ujjain."

"I had read somewhere that a drop had spilled on Kashi too. You corrected me today."

"There are many pilgrims who think like you. Now this event is commemorated once in every three years by the Kumbh Mela, at each tirtha in turn. And here the Kumbh is held once in every twelve years, which is the greatest and holiest of all."

"I'd heard of the Naga Sadhus who come down from the mountains and forests to attend this, Mela."

"Bilkul sahi. The Maha Kumbh Mela is the largest religious congregation in India, attended by millions. It is a month long fair. The jyotishis have decided the Kumbhayog, the holy time for bathing. The first to hit the water is by legions of Naga Sadhus or Naga Babas, who cover their naked bodies with ash and wear hair in long dreadlocks."

"They come to the Ganga Sagar Mela as well in our Paschim Bangal."

"Ji haan. Now look over there", the navwala pointed towards the east, " you see that harey rang ka pani?"

"Yes, yes" Mrunal responded while switching on her video camera,

"Those are waters of Yamuna Maiya, and this one is of Ganga Maiya, flowing towards Kashi nagri. And Saraswati nadi is unseen but it is believed to run underground."

The boat reached the mid-river point, where the priests perched on small platforms performing yagyas, reciting mantras from the Rig Veda and assisting devots in their ritual ablutions in the shallow water. Mrunal got down from the boat and let off the diya in the silver foil to the holy waters and finally took a small dip in the sangham. It soothed her mind, body and soul. She wrapped herself in a gerua namawali and recited:

"*Om jaba kusuma sankhasam,*

Kashyapeyang mahadhvatim,

Dhantaring sarwa paap abhnam, pranata hashmi divakaram,

Om bhagwate Sri Suryay Namah:"

The serene ambience of Triveni indeed weaves elements of sight, scent, and sound into a mesmerizing visual poetry. Here, the holy fire of Yagyas whispers to the sacred fragrance of incense sticks, mingling with the soft petals of roses adrift upon the water's surface.

"How do you feel?" the naukawala asked Mrunal on her way back to the Ghat,

"Relaxed and fresh."

"Now look at your east, do you see that imarat?"

"That looks like a fort!"

"It was built by Mughal Badshah Akbar."

"Wait wait. This is the Allahbad fort, right? I'd read about this fort long ago. It is mentioned by Abul Fazl in the Akbarnama as well."

"Local Prayagwal Brahmins tell a tale of Akbar's struggles to build this fort. Each attempt was foiled by the sand's instability. They advised him that only a human sacrifice could solve the problem. A brave local Brahmin volunteered this issue, leading Akbar to grant his descendants, the Prayagwals, the exclusive right to serve the pilgrims at Sangam. Another legend claims that Akbar was once Mukunda Brahmachari, a Hindu ascetic, who, overcome with guilt after accidentally ingesting a cow's hair, took his own life. This act, it's said, led to his rebirth as a non-Hindu, driving him to construct a fort at this Sangam."

"What about the British? How did they use this fort?"

"For Angrez, this fort was most probably a grand depot for their military sources after the Nawab of Oudh, Sadat Ali Khan ceded the fort to the East India Company since he was financially strapped."

"This fort is comparatively larger than the other forts built by Akbar. Really, it's an architectural masterpiece of their zamana. By the way, chachaji, you made my journey more beautiful with this conversation."

"This is my work, madamji."

As she rode her Tonga towards the Nirala Chat center through the Civil Lines, known for its tasty vegan food, including gulab jamun and various types of chat, she passed by the main gate of Prayag Sangeet Samiti. This place held dear memories from her childhood. Mrunal had taken talim in Hindustani classical music and Bharatnatyam under this institute from her elementary school days until 7th grade. She could learn only five forms of Ragas—Yaman, Kaafi, Bhairav, Vilaval, and Khamaj—before her asthma attacks forced her to stop with her practice, including her dance performances at Rabindra Sadan in Kolkata.. This chapter of her life echoes in few of Tagore's lines from his poem, "Rupnaraner Kuley", which say…

"The truth, as arduous as it may be,

I cherished its trials,

For it never deceives.

Life, a crucible of sorrow's fire,

In truth's grasp, discovers its worth,

In death, settling all debts it may acquire."

After having a plate of aloo chat at Nirala and drinking a glass of lassi garnished with lots of dry fruits and malai on the top, she left the Tonga and took a shared toto from Sardar Patel Marg to the Saraswati ghat for a evening walk. While strolling through the garden which lead to the river bank, Mrunal called her mother,

"Did you do any puja at the Sangham?"

"Yes maa. Had an interesting talk with the maajhi too."

"You're a history buff and your aura also attracts such people. Where are you now and when will you go back to the ashram?"

"Saraswati ghat, it seems to be newly built to attract more tourists. It has beautiful Lotus shaped domes, similar to the ones at Mumbai airport with beautiful wall murals illustrating palkis, marriage, men playing shehnai, and seems to have beautiful kalamkari motifs at the edges of the staircase as well. Yamuna nadi flows right in front of it. I wanted to breathe for some time, so I decided to come here. Heard about this place from the Tonga wala"

"You remember those lines of that Bhajan 'Ya mohana'?"

"Meera di had trained me well in this particular Bhajan, I do…

'Yamuna ke teerey dhenu charawata,

Bansi mein gaawe, meethi vaani'.

This one na?"

"Yes, Maa Yamuna is really old. Both the Rigveda and Atharvaveda mention her. Throughout history, many empires were centered around this Ganga-Yamuna basin, including the Gupta, Shunga, and Maurya empires. Even the Kushanas and Mughals had their capital cities here, such as Mathura and Agra."

"Indeed ma, even in South India, depictions of the Ganges and Yamuna can be seen alongside shrines of the Chalukyas and Rashtrakutas, as well as on their royal seals. Before them, the Chola Empire also incorporated the river into their architectural designs. For example, the Three River Goddess shrine, situated next to the Kailash rock-cut Temple at Ellora, showcases the Ganges flanked by the Yamuna and Saraswati. ."

"Ei Shona. How far is Mathura from Allahabad?"

"Not much maa, why?"

"You can perform Gau seva over there. Its Kartik mahina, an extremely pious month for visiting Vrindavan."

"I'll have to extend my leave for a few more days then. Don't know if the college authority would grant me or not. Oh well, I can perform Baba's batshorik over there this way. It's on 17th naa?"

"Hmm"

"God really has his own plans. Thank you maa. Really thank you."

"You're a dutiful daughter beta. We never needed a son, because we had you. You're enough."

"Why does your voice sound so low? Cheer up. Well, I'm thinking of visiting Anand Bhawan tomorrow. You know right, that it was the residence of Pandit Nehru?"

"It's a government holiday tomorrow. I feel it would remain closed."

"Oh children's day!"

"Yes, my child."

Both giggled.

"I've recorded a few videos. I'll send them after I reach the ashram. Bye ma."

"Take care beta."

The pink hues of the staircase and domes blended seamlessly with the evening twilight. The gentle breeze of the Yamuna tousled Mrunal's hair as the sun dipped behind the distant bridge, peeking through the canopy of trees at the ghat. Mrunal's hair resembled brush strokes dipped in twilight, and her dangling oxidized jhumkas swayed hypnotically with the evening air. While watching the fading rays of the sun and the river welcoming dusk, Mrunal plugged in her earphones, played Raag Bageshri and closed her eyes. The lines sung by Mangal Mishra harmonized perfectly with the view in front...

"Ae Ri pawan, ja ja zara de, Mora sandeshwa."

Mrunal spent the next day getting ready for the seminar. She revised her part many times in front of the small wooden dressing mirror. She chose an off-white schiffli blouse with a laced Peter Pan collar, pearl earrings, a light blue organza saree with floral prints, and jasmine-scented itar. While ironing her blouse, she remembered a two liner from the YourQuote App..

"I realise I look gorgeous in Maa's sarees now, as more than cotton or silk, they are stitched with sweat and sacrifice."

Train To Mathura

"Maharaj Ji, is there any car facility from the ashram to go the station?"

"Yes, another Bengali family also have their train to Haridwar, so they are moving towards the station as well. But you've to go right now along with since you won't find any vehicle after 8pm from here."

"I don't have any problem, where's the family?'

In the courtyard outside the Shiv temple, there was a Bengali family of five: two men with their wives and a small boy wearing a monkey tupi and woollens, munching on Joynogorer mowa. The head Maharaj introduced Mrunal to the family.

"She's Mrunal Ganguly, a professor and psychologist. She had a lecture at Allahabad University today and is catching a train to Mathura around 11:30, so just see if you could…"

"Your saree is stunning. Did you get it from Mohinimohan Kanjilal?" one of the ladies inquired, sparking a conversation with Mrunal.

Indeed, any Bengali, especially from Kolkata, would always tend to prefer Mohinimohan Kanjilal for shopping sarees.

"No no, burrabazar saree patti. You get it at a wholesale rate over there."

"You look like a Hyderabadi princess in this attire, especially because of those pearl studs. You really radiate the aura of a psychologist"

"You're gorgeous too"

The conversation evolved into a cultural exchange inside the 7-seater Innova car as it moved through the quiet roads of Prayagraj.

"I'm a classical singer by profession. We're on our way to Haridwar to offer a puja for my husband's new job. He's a civil engineer but was unemployed for the past 2 years. At that time, I supported my family by giving music lessons and performing at concerts. I was fortunate to be a disciple of Girija Devi, which is why I was here to attend her concert. So, we planned the entire trip around that." the lady added on…

"Girija Deviji? I used to learn classical music from one of her associates, Dr. Aditi Chakraborty. But couldn't specialize in Thumri alike her."

"Girija deviji is indeed the queen of Thumri. You know, after guruji made her first debut in in 1949 on All India Radio Allahabad, she had faced opposition from her mother and grandmother because it was traditionally believed that no upper-class woman should perform publicly. Her father, Ramdeo Rai was a Zamindar, so you understand why..."

"Quite a natural scene for women in the early years of post-independence era."

"But interestingly, it was her father who made Guruji take lessons in singing khyal and tappa from vocalist and sarangi player Sarju Prasad Misra. She started with her talim from the age of 5 itself. In our Kolkata, she is a member of ITC Sangeet Research Academy."

"A queen of Indian classical music indeed. By the way, tappa originated in the Banaras gharana, isn't it?"

" No, actually from the folk songs of the camel riders in Punjab, until it was refined and introduced to the imperial court of the Mughal Emperor Muhammad Shah and later by Shori Mian, a court singer of Asaf-Ud-Dowlah, Nawab of Awadh."

"Baba had once told me a story about how tappa gayaki had started in Bengal. Back in the late 1800s and early 1900s, rich people and regular folks both liked listening to tappa. Another type of tappa called baithaki style became popular with the help of zamindar. They used to host gatherings in their jalsaghar and baithak-khanas. Also, I think it was Ramnidhi Gupta & Kalidas Chattopadhyay who created Bengali tappa, which later became known as Nidhubabu's tappa. Bengali tappa was famous for mixing humor and artistry, often including funny English phrases to entertain British officials during the British rule. But those English lines secretly criticized the British government, although they were cleverly disguised so they wouldn't get in trouble. You know that song? The one that goes "Let me go, ohe dwari, tumi kader kuler bou..." Ramkumar Chattopadhyay babu translated it humorously as "Madam, whose family you belong to..."

"Yes, these men also contributed to our freedom struggle in a unique way. You can conquer a soil, but never it's art. Noibo, noibocho..."

"Ah, Nana ronger din."

"Oh, so you got it. By the way, how was your lecture?"

"I was invited as a guest lecturer to a seminar for the first time, that too by the Oxford of East. When I stepped into the Vizianagaram hall, it felt like I was entering a royal palace with a mix of Indo-Saracenic, Egyptian, and Gothic styles of architecture. From a stone inscription outside the entrance, I discovered that it was designed by none other than Sir William Emerson, the same architect behind Kolkata's Victoria Memorial!"

"Ore baba, a mini union of UP and Bengal then!"

"Really, I mean really. And to surprise me even more, the inscription further read that initially, the Allahabad University used to function under the University of Calcutta!"

"Waah waah. I never knew that UP and Bengal are so intricately connected!"

"They are... in lots of aspects..."

"What was the topic of the seminar?"

"Neurological basis of human memory and psycho-oncology. I had to address a certain portion of human memory highlighting it's recently posited models and theories by psychologists from all across the globe and their relationship with neurological findings of human cognitive functioning. "

"Hmm... that's huge."

"Quite a bit. But what mattered to me was the honour that I received as an external and the way I was received with a beautiful bouquet. Trust me, it melted my heart. I felt as if I'd survived to achieve this."

"You're an extra ordinary woman."

"So are you. A lot more than me. Earning bread for the family all alone, looking after a small child, and supporting your husband financially.... That's love, that's how a family should be."

The car stopped outside the Allahabad Junction. After exchanging mobile numbers with each other, both the ladies departed for their respective platforms.

The scenery at Allahabad station at 8:30 at night differed from the city, which was asleep except for the occasional blare of truck horns and the sparse traffic on the main road. CRPF Jawans patrolled the platforms with two to three German Shepherd dogs, ensuring a high level of safety for solo travelers like Mrunal. She settled in the ladies' waiting room,which was well-equipped with modern conveniences like four charging stations, a TV, and a display board. A diverse group of women occupied the space: some rested on the floor with beautiful lehraiya-styled ghunghat covering their faces, while others, including students remained engrossed in their laptops and few elderly widows with a tilak on their foreheads and tulsi kanthi around their necks, softly chanted the name of Govind Ji, caressing their rosary. One of them sat beside Mrunal, reading "Mirabai ke dohey" and constantly counting her rosary beads. Her face bore a striking resemblance to Khushwant Singh's description of his grandmother in the story "The Portrait of a Lady," which said:

"Her silver locks were scattered untidily over her pale, puckered face, and her lips constantly moved in inaudible prayer.... She was like the winter landscape in the mountains, an expanse of pure white serenity breathing peace and serenity."

"Mashi, what are you reading?" Mrunal asked her,

" You know MiraBai?", the vidhwa answered.

"Yes, the Maharani Of Chittor who left her rajpath for puja archana of Shri Krishna."

"Nahi, it doesn't end here, see this is the problem with everyone. Nobody talks about her contributions to sangeet and sahitya.", the widow protested while keeping back her rosary beads in a small cotton bag.

"Arrey mashi, I know that she was a poet. But I haven't read any of her works till now. Whatever I know about her is from an old biopic which had Hema Malini in its lead role. Tell me something more about her, I would love to hear.."

"It's a long story, suno tab.. Mirabai was a princess born into a Rathore Rajput royal family in Kudki. Aam admi often highlight her as a lady who loitered around for Lord Krishna, but they often forget to focus on her fearless disregard for social and family conventions. She unwillingly married Bhoj Raj, the Yuvraj of Mewar. He was badly wounded in one of the ongoing wars with the Delhi Sultanate in around, uhm.. 1518, and he died from battle wounds after two years. Both her father and father-in-law, Rana Sanga, died a few days after their defeat in the Battle of Khanwa against Babur, the first Mughal Emperor. Her in-laws tried to assassinate her multiple times, like sending Meera a glass of poison and telling her it was nectar. "

" I can recollect this story from Anup Jalota's Bhajan, arre that one...

'Rana ne vish diya, mano amrit Diya' "

"You know that song... *Payo ji maine, Ram ratan dhan payo?*"

"My mother used to play these bhajans on every Sunday morning."

"It was composed by Meerabai. These are known as Rajasthani padas. This is how she contributed to the Bhakti movement of solavi shatabdi. The bhaktamal poem which was written in our Brajboli gives short biographies of more than 200 bhaktas, and it mentions Meerabai as one of them. And this bhakti movement has been considered an influential social reformation in Hinduism. It provided an individual-focused alternative path to spirituality regardless of one's birth or gender, which originated in South India and gained prominence through the poems and teachings of the Vaishnava Alvars and Shaiva Nayanars before spreading to North India."

"Mashi, I had one question. "

"Wait na, I've Katha Upanishad in my jhola. I'll give you; you can read more about Bhakti movement in it. And she contributed a lot to shastriya sangeet by composing various ragas and tikas, like Raag Govind, Raag Soratha, Meera Ki Malhar, Mira Padavali, and govind tika. You know, her poetry is also written in Adi Granth Sahib of the Sikhs."

The lady began searching for the book In her off-white, slightly tattered jhola and handed the book of dohas to Mrunal to hold. As she flipped through the pages, one of the translations read:

"After making me fall for you so hard, where are you going?

Until the day I see you, no repose: my life, like a fish washed on shore, flails in agony.

For your sake I'll make myself a yogini, I'll hurl myself to death on the saw of Kashi.

*Mira's God is the clever Mountain Lifter, and I am his, a slave to his lotus fee*t.

—Mira Bai, Translated by John Stratton Hawley"

A Portrait Of Meerabai

"Mashi, why did Meera call herself a Yogini in this poem?"

The widow read the Hindi translation on the right page and said,

"The characteristic of her poetry is complete surrender. Krishna is a yogi and lover, and she herself is a yogini, ready to take her place by his side in a spiritual marital bliss."

"Mashi, how do you know so much?"

"I was married off at the age of 12 to a wealthy family in Khuri, Rajasthan. Despite being expected to focus solely on household chores, I had a keen interest in learning and studying. Fortunately, my bapusa had taught me how to read; he used to work at the newspaper factory. However, my in-laws never permitted me to read. They only expected me to handle the stove and grind spices. Yet, my husband deeply cared for me. He would secretly provide me with newspapers and small scriptures to read, hiding them from my mother-in-law. Sadly, our destiny separated us... what to do.."

"Don't you have any children?"

"I have a son who has become a Brahmachari monk and now runs an ashram in Kashi. I am currently returning to my Vidhwa Ashram in Vrindavan. I prefer to reside there, amidst akhand kirtan and braj ki mitti. And let me tell you, don't think that I beg around like other vidhwas of my age. I sell diyas and cotton strands for 40 rupees outside Banke Bihari Ji temple, offering various styles and designs. Here, take one."

She gifted a beautiful Lotus shaped Diya to Mrunal with a small cotton strand.

" Mashi, can I take a selfie with you?"

"What?"

"I mean, a picture. You're like my grandma, she was just like you, always keen to learn and study from whatever piece of information she found, even the dictionary. She never wasted her time watching TV serials, like other old Bengali women. You remind me so much of her."

A tear dropped from the corner of Mrunal's right eye. The old widow hugged her and patted her back, planting a gentle kiss on her forehead.

"Naa betaji, don't cry. Take my number, we will talk over call from now. And here's my son's card, if you ever visit Kashi, you can stay at his ashram."

"What's the name of your ashram?"

"Tarini Vidhwa Ashram."

"I'm also going to Vrindavan, I'll visit you once I'm there."

"I would've asked you to stay in my ashram itself with me, but our head in charge doesn't allow any unmarried woman to stay."

"It's okay mashi. I've talked with the Maharaj of Ram Krishna Mission, Mathura. I'll be getting a small bunglow for my stay. But we can go together from the station na?"

"No, I have to meet my cousin in Kasganj. Will get down from the train before you But call me if you have any trouble."

In India, people are like the colorful splashes of Holi, diverse yet united in creating and celebrating friendship. As the train arrived at platform number 1, there was a buzz among passengers near the RAC and waiting list areas. Inside the dimly lit general compartment, typical of trains coming from Howrah, passengers were fast asleep. Mrunal struggled with her phone's flashlight to find her seat—common occurrence on Indian train rides.

"Excuse me, ma'am, but that's my seat," a young man's voice called out to Mrunal as she adjusted her suitcase under the berth.

"Ji wait. Let me lock my trolley."

"Sure sure, I said it to avoid any misunderstanding. Take your time. Can I help you?"

"Can you hold the flashlight for me?"

Mrunal then asked an elderly local couple about the train's schedule and the station before Mathura junction since her mobile network had died, preventing her from checking the train status on the IRCTC app.

"Don't worry beta, Hathras city will come before Mathura. This train is usually late. So, sleep in peace, we will inform you." The old lady assured her.

"Madam, I'll be getting down at Mathura junction..", the guy finally spoke after their conversation stopped.

"Oh Thank God."

"Are you travelling all alone?"

"Yes, I'm going to Vrindavan to perform a few annual rites for my father."

"I've never seen any girl performing the last rites for her parents, you're the first person I have encountered to do so. Really... "

"Most of the Bengali families also don't allow their daughters to perform these rites. But my family is an exceptional case."

"Are you from Kolkata?"

"Yes.. a professor and psychologist based over there. I'm planning to shift to Mumbai in a year. My card ... "

Mrunal briefly introduced herself and her extra ordinary reason for travelling in general boggies instead of AC coaches.

"I'm Jayesh, currently in my final year pursuing a B. Arch degree at IIT BHU. My home is in Vrindavan, near the Radha Raman Mandir. I must say, you truly possess commendable qualities."

"Thank you, but I don't know anything about Brajdham. Tell me about a few temples in the morning, I would love to visit them."

"Sure didi…"

The following morning, Mrunal found out that the train was running 4 hours behind schedule. She quickly called her mother to inform her about the delay, only to receive a barrage of scolding in return.

"Who had asked you to travel in the general compartment?" her mother shouted over the phone.

"Maa, the entire train is late. Not just the general coach."

"I'm not talking about it. Your tickets weren't confirmed. You're travelling alone. Anything could happen."

"No, not really. I've got really genuine co-passengers. Don't worry about me."

The network died before she could finish her conversation. Mrunal ate the dosa she had packed from Jaiswal Dosa Centre the previous day in Prayagraj, which she shared with the young man and the elderly couple.

"It was your mom over the call na?" Jayesh asked…

"Yes, how do you know?"

"Only Indian moms have this rare talent of making a mountain out of a mole."

Both laughed over a sip of chai.

"So you asked me about the temples last night. But I'm telling you in advance, that you won't be able to cover all of them, because Vrindavan has more than 4000 temples."

"I've less time in my hands as well, but tell me the important and unique ones. First start with the one situated near your house."

"Okay, so Radha Raman ji ki mandir is counted as one of the seven most revered ancient temples of Vrindavan along with Radha Vallabh Temple, Radha Damodar Temple, Radha Madanmohan Temple, Radha Govindji Temple, Radha Shyamsundar Temple and Radha Gokulnandan Temple. Radha Raman Ji Ki

Mandir has the original Shaligram deity of Shri Krishna and Radha Rani. It was built over 500 years ago by Gopala Bhatta Goswami. When Gopala Bhatta Gosvami was thirty, he came to Vrindavan. After Chaitanya Mahaprabhu left, he felt very sad. One fine day in a dream, Kanha came and told him, "If you want to see Me, go to Nepal."

In Nepal, Gopala Bhatta bathed in the famous Kali-Gandaki River. While filling his waterpot from the river, he was surprised to find several Shaligram Shilas entering it. Even after he put them back in the river, they returned to his pot. On the full moon day, after offering food to his Shaligram Shilas, Gopala Bhatta covered them with a basket. During the night, he rested for a while. Early in the morning, he went to bathe in the Yamuna river. When he returned, he uncovered the Shaligrams to worship them and saw a Deity of Krishna playing the flute among them. There were now only eleven Shilas and a Deity. The "Damodara shila" had transformed into the beautiful three-fold bending form of Tri-Bhangananda-Krishna. This is how Radha Ramanji merged as a perfectly formed deity from a sacred Shaligram Shila."

"My music teacher used to have a shaligram Narayan in her place. She used to worship it a lot and called it jagrat."

"Shaligram shila is sakshat Narayan. The next place for a must visit is Banke Bihari Ji. His murti is the combined form of Radha Krishna, manifested by Vrindavan musician and saint Swami Haridas who is believed to be the incarnation of Lalita gopi, a close associate of Radha Krishna in their Goloka."

"Sant Haridas was the guru of Tansen right?"

"Yes. Banke means 'bent', and 'Bihari' means 'enjoyer'. This is how Kṛiṣhṇa, who is bent in three places, got the name "Banke Bihari". According to Sri Brahma-samhita, Brahma dev had also described Kanhaji…

'I worship Govinda, the primeval Lord, round whose neck is swinging a garland of flowers beautified with the moon-locket, whose two hands are adorned with the flute and jewelled ornaments, who always revels in pastimes of love, whose graceful threefold-bending form of Shyamasundara is eternally manifest.'

By the way, you will be allowed only a jhalak darshan of the murti, the pujaris don't allow you to stare at it for long.

Also, don't forget to visit Nidhivan and Vanshivat. We believe that Radha and Krishna still perform Maharas in both places on every purnima. And you can go for a boat ride and explore the ghats. Keep gopeshwar Mahadev and Jaipur mandir too in your checklist."

<u>*A Few Pictures of Vrindavan including: Keshi Ghat, Jaipur Mandir and a glimpse of Kunjagalis*</u>

"I don't know if I'll be able to cover so many in a day. But I'll try my level best. "

"Try to hire a Toto, it can take you for a tour. Booking a private car is a waste of money."

"I don't prefer private cars.."

"Oh yes, the extra ordinary Bengali girl."

Mrunal smiled at him.

"A few metres away from the exit of the baki bihari temple complex, you'll find lots of chat bhandar in line. Try alu tikki chat over there and kesar dudh outside Gopeshwar Mahadev. You can pack some anguri petha for home as well, they are famous in our Mathura and Agra since the rule of Badshah Shah Jahan."

"Oh, so it was Shah Jahan who introduced Petha?"

"Yes. He asked his chefs to make a unique dessert that is as pure and white like the Taj Mahal. The royal chefs worked hard and came up with a new invention called Petha. Due to its ingredients, comprising of fruit, sugar and water, it is considered the purest dessert in the world. It is not cooked on a regular cooking fire, only coal fire is used. The one made in Agra even has a Geographical Indication tag to certify its place of origin."

"Bapre!"

"Many varieties of Petha have come up in the market to cater to the demand and changing palate of the locals. Nowadays, buyers can choose from kesar petha, angoori petha to chocolate petha and paan petha... The list goes on... "

"You know, the biggest historians and tour guides are the locals of any place. "

The gentleman blushed while looking down at his phone.

"My father will be coming to the station to receive me. Would you like to meet him? Also, do you provide therapy sessions online?"

"I would be happy to meet him. And I do conduct online sessions."

"I'm passing through a really bad phase in my life. My mother passed away a few months back, and I'm extremely stressed out about my internship and job. I wanted to seek help, but it just didn't happen out of the blue."

"I'm there, don't worry."

Mathura

The train arrived at Mathura Junction at 9 a.m. Mrunal exchanged a warm goodbye with her new client and his old father. As she traveled through the roads of Mathura in the auto, memories of her childhood trip to Gaya flooded back – the pigs, cows, roads, fields, and the sun felt familiar, but there were new additions like old temples, peacocks, and monkeys to the scenario. Mrunal had already gotten permission from the head of the Ram Krishna Mission to stay at their guest house via email. The Mission's complex was grand, with trees lining the paths and a large hospital across from the guest house. The Ram Krishna Mission Hospital still provides free care to thousands of patients in Mathura, a remarkable service in today's world. Their motto is "Serving Man is Serving God," which guides all their activities.

Swami Vivekananda established the Ramakrishna Mission in honor of his guru and raised funds for the Mission from various sources. The non-profit organization has been serving humankind for almost 125 years now. It has a two-fold purpose: to spread the teachings of the Hindu philosophy of Vedanta and to uplift the oppressed masses of the country. Swami Vivekananda believed strongly in the potential of youth to change the world. He urged Indian youth to educate themselves and emphasized that service should be the focus of their lives. He once said, "It is a privilege to serve mankind, for this is the worship of God. God is here, in all these human souls. He is the soul of man." He coined a new term, Daridra Narayana – 'God in the poor and the lowly,' instilling a sense of religious duty towards the poor.

Mrunal left the ashram and bought a dozen of guavas, pears and bananas. Then, she hired a Toto to take her to visit the temples for 100 rupees per hour. As the vehicle drove through the Kunj Galis, they passed by beautiful blue houses, reminiscent of those in Jodhpur, Rajasthan. Some of them were festooned with wall paintings depicting tales from Krishna Katha, like kaliya Daman and makhan chori. Mrunal noticed a few weak calves with bones sticking out, indicating they hadn't been given much food by their owners, likely due to neglect.

"Aren't they given proper food? Stop the Toto."

Mrunal got down and fed bananas and pears to the calves and patted their backs.

"Some calves and cows are only kept for milk. They are not properly looked after. What to do, it's their destiny.", the Toto driver insisted…

"Why keep animals if you cannot look after them, isn't it?"

"Irony is, Vrindavan is also called Golok or Gokul."

As Mrunal beheld the vista afore her, wondrous Rajasthani architectural marvels unfolded, none more bewitching than the temples themselves. Most of these structures were erstwhile havelis and palaces bestowed by Rajput maharajas, dedicated to their deities' service. Despite enduring the ravages of foreign interlopers, many of these temples have been painstakingly restored over time.

Among these gems, the Banke Bihari ji temple stood out, its Rajasthani architecture resplendent in its beauty; The Radha Vallabh temple crafted from red sandstone in the year 1585, and the majestic Jaipur mandir, enveloped by the verdant ambiance of trees, commissioned by Maharaj Sawai Madhao Singh in 1917. Few are privy to the knowledge that the Maharaja engineered the construction of railway lines between Mathura and Vrindavan expressly for the transportation of hefty sandstone and other materials essential for erecting this sumptuous temple. Astonishing in appearance and exquisite in design, the architect had reinvigorated the aesthetic of the Mughal emperor's edifices and palaces. It was meticulously crafted with original marble and sandstone, even incorporating sturdy rocks to impart a distinctiveness to this temple. The craftsmanship employed in its construction was unparalleled, evident to any visitor who beheld its splendor, both in skill and the wealth expended to realize it. The Maharaja's profound devotion to Radharani led to the dedication of this temple to Radha-Madhava ji. Massive pillars were erected to support this magnificent structure and its ornate doors. Comprising three chambers—one opening to the north towards Shri Anand-Bihariji, another to the central altar of Shri Radha-Madhavji, and the third to the south towards Shri Nitya-Gopalji and other divine deities. After offering prayers for her father at Gopeshwar Mahadev mandir and feeding the cows and goats outside, Mrunal strolled towards Vanshivat. Within its precincts, a grand banyan tree stood amidst the chessboard-patterned floor, surrounded by wall carvings depicting the Ashtasakhis wearing traditional Rajasthani ghagras, encircling a lotus motif. A pair of majestic peafowls glided into the complex, their elegant movements harmonizing with the tranquil breeze wafting from the Yamuna, caressing their vibrant plumage. The entire scene exuded an aura of pristine purity akin to Sanskrit verses delicately woven into its fabric, redolent of roses nestled amidst the pages of shayars, watered by the timeless gaze of antiquity. It seemed as if the phad painting of her fellow traveler en route to Allahabad had sprung to life before her very eyes. Mrunal approached the river bank with her excitement palpable as she readied herself for a boat journey through the ghats. The boatman guided the vessel through the emerald depths of the river, passing by Keshi Ghat, Kalia Daman Ghat, Govind Ghat, and Cheer Ghat along the parikrama marg. Each ghat held remnants of ancient temples and havelis, their whispers echoing tales of times long past. At the end of the secluded pathways (kunjgali), each structure emanated an essence woven with the stories of its journey through time's corridors. The sky above and the waters of the Yamuna below have always shared a common bond—they have beheld history, bearing witness to the rise and fall of empires along their banks. In the annals spanning from the Vedic epochs unto the zenith of Anglo-Saxon dominion, Uttar Pradesh has stood as a beacon of cultural opulence, weaving the golden strands of classical melodies, courtly dances, epicurean delights, regal vestments, imperial majesty, and ethereal spirituality through the loom of time. Mrunal casted her gaze aloft, where the heavens bespoke the covenant of impending rains. Her vision then alighted upon the serpentine flow of the Yamuna, transmuting her orbs into glistening dewdrops akin to pearls adorning a peacock's resplendent train, engaging her lens in a tacit discourse reminiscent of the dulcet sonnets of Rag Megh Malhar—a language that doth resonate with every Indian maiden, be she ensconced within the sanctum of her urban city life or amidst the verdant fields of her ancestral demesne.

After 3 months...

At Mrunal's private chamber in Kolkata, sunlight streamed through the European-styled tilt and turn windows. Against one wall stood a sturdy black wooden bookshelf, its shelves filled with an array of books on history, art, and human cognitive system. Perched among them were bonsai plants. Their miniature leaves swayed gently in the breeze that drifted through the open window, carrying a subtle scent of incense. Outside, the roads of Shyambazar hummed with activity thereby creating a soundtrack which added to the list of extraneous variables in Mrunal's experimental designs. Portraits of Sigmund Freud, Abraham Maslow and Carl Jung hung above the shelf. Mrunal leaned back in her chair as her thoughts drifted back to her recent journey through Uttar Pradesh. She had returned home with a renewed sense of purpose, eager to integrate the lessons she had learned into her psychology practice. She had just finished an online therapy session with a client when there was a knock on the door.

"Come in," she called, her curiosity piqued.

She looked up to see that it was the same young man she had met in her train to Mathura.

"Hello again Jayesh," Mrunal said, offering him a warm smile. "What brings you to Kolkata?"

The young man hesitated for a moment before speaking. "I'm here for an internship," he explained, his voice tinged with uncertainty. "I've been working at an architecture firm for the past few months.. just trying to gain practical experience before I graduate."

"Is it the same internship you told me about in the train?"

"Yes.."

Mrunal nodded in understanding, gesturing for him to take a seat. As they talked, Jayesh opened up about the challenges he had faced during his internship, the pressure to perform and the fear of failure weighing heavily on his mind.

"I've been feeling overwhelmed lately," he admitted, his voice barely above a whisper. "I thought coming here might help me to gain some perspective, to find a way to cope with the stress I'm passing through these days."

She could sense his struggle, the internal conflict raging within him as he grappled with the demands of his profession and the expectations placed upon him by others, including the work politics.

"Would you like to continue our therapy session in person?" Mrunal gently made the offer, knowing that sometimes, a face-to-face connection could make all the difference. She knew that traditional therapy techniques alone would not be enough to help him find relief. Drawing on her recent experiences, Mrunal suggested him to try something different.

"Would you like to explore your feelings through art?" she asked, gesturing to the easel and paints set up in the corner of the room.

Under Mrunal's guidance, he began to paint, his brush moving across the white sheet with a sense of purpose and intensity. As he worked, Mrunal encouraged him to express himself more freely, to let go of his inhibitions and allow his emotions to flow.

Together, she delved deeper into the depths of his psyche, uncovering the root causes of his depression and exploring other strategies for coping and healing.

Through the process of art therapy, the young man began to find solace and strength, his inner landscape gradually shifted from darkness to light.

In the weeks and months that followed, Mrunal continued to refine her approach to therapy, drawing inspiration from the stories of the remarkable women she had met during her journey throughout Uttar Pradesh. She found that by integrating elements of storytelling and art into her sessions, she could create a space for her patients to explore their innermost thoughts and feelings, to connect with their cultural heritage, and to find hope and healing in the midst of adversity.

Her chamber transformed into a place where history, art, and psychology converged to create moments of profound connection and transformation. While she sat in her office, surrounded by the soothing rustle of paintbrushes, Mrunal knew that she had found her true calling, a calling that would guide her on a lifelong journey of discovery and healing.

About the Author

Annapurna Debnath

Annapurna Debnath (b. 2004) is a student at Gokhale Memorial Girls' College affiliated with the University of Calcutta in Kolkata, West Bengal. She is a published poet and is presently pursuing an Honours degree in Psychology.

www.ingramcontent.com/pod-product-compliance
Lightning Source LLC
LaVergne TN
LVHW041626070526
838199LV00052B/3258